PRACTICAL PROGRAMMING

£1-60

PRACTICAL PROGRAMMING

Peter Pipe

ROBERT E. KRIEGER PUBLISHING COMPANY
HUNTINGTON, NEW YORK
1977

For
Molly

who quieted

Gabrielle, Keeble, Ennis, Ian, *and* Elise

Original Edition 1966
Reprint 1977

Printed and Published by
ROBERT E. KRIEGER PUBLISHING CO., INC.
645 NEW YORK AVENUE
HUNTINGTON, NEW YORK 11743

Copyright © 1966 by
HOLT, RINEHART, & WINSTON
Reprinted by Arrangement

Printed in the United States of America

Library of Congress Cataloging in Publication Data

Pipe, Peter.
   Practical programming.
   Reprint of the ed. published by Holt, Rinehart and Winston, New York.
   Includes index.
   1. Programmed instruction I. Title.
LB 1028.5.P53 1977 371.39'442 76-27984
ISBN 0-88275-468-8

Preface

Teaching people to talk about something is fine if that is what you are setting out to do. But it is a poor substitute for teaching them how to do things when *doing* is the skill required. The field of programmed instruction provides a good example of this double standard. It is new, apparently simple, and laden with promise. Understandably, many people want to learn to program. They study the literature and some even attend classes. But in far too many cases they end up with an ability to talk about programmed instruction and an uneasy feeling that they still could not write a program.

It seems to me that there are several reasons for this. The field is full of conflicting opinions and loyalties. There are those who advocate linear programming and those who adhere to branching programming. There are some who want to spell it "programming" and some who prefer "programing." Some banish the programming process to the interesting province of folklore called common sense. Others invest it with mysticism and, according to their individual talents, would have you believe that it is either a science or an art, unattainable to those denied formal, ritualistic training.

The literature reflects these divisions and also is deficient in its treatment of some aspects of programming. As a result, the beginner who must rely on the literature (or on a teacher whose knowledge is limited to what is written down) finds himself in two kinds of trouble. First, his concept of what is important is short of some vital information. Second, he has concentrated on the wrong things *for a beginner,*

This book attempts to overcome the difficulties that face a beginner. It sets down some procedures that, although not particularly unusual, are hard to come by elsewhere. They are aimed at getting you started on program writing as quickly and painlessly as possible. I will not go so far as to say that one learns about programming only by programming. But I do believe that you should learn to use the techniques discussed here and that you should then try to write a program before you dig deeper into theory. Given that first experience, the technicalities of why and how programmers break information into little steps will no longer seem so mysterious. You will find in programmed instruction a good deal from that scientific grab bag called psychology and you will see in a good program a fair amount of art. But there is also in programming a great deal of the common experience of humanity. If you have practical experience or new ideas, you may have something useful to contribute to a program.

I would not want you to read into that last paragraph an implication that everybody can and should write programs. I feel very strongly that programming is not an activity in which most people become competent. On the other hand, I feel just as strongly that everybody concerned with teaching (whether in the academic world or outside it) should write at least one program. The process can provide valuable insights. Setting aside questions of who can or who should write programs, it seems to me that many people are going to involve themselves with programming simply because they have a job to do and a program looks like a good way to do it.

This book confines itself to the practical, an orientation which may annoy those of dedicated scientific or artistic integrity because it will suggest that some of the "laws" and "rules" by which they work are not rock-founded articles of faith, but positions on a tortuous, groping path toward truth. It may also annoy the professing realists who hold that the writing of a program consists of chopping a narrative into little pieces (sentence-size pieces for one school of thought, paragraph-size pieces for another) and then putting in questions after each piece.[1] While the

[1] It is true that programs often look like fragments interspersed with questions. It is possible to generate a program using this technique. It is even possible that somebody will learn from such a program since students will persist in thinking, no matter how they are abused.

actions of the purists sometimes arouse my sympathy with the realists, the latter's approach is not, in the long run, an efficient one.

Besides dealing with practical matters, the book differs from much of the literature in this field in yet another way. For the most part, it avoids the usual broad statements about the applications of programmed instruction, the mechanics of frame writing,[2] or the reports on studies (an interesting mixture, these, of scientific detachment and wishful thinking). It avoids these areas because, in my opinion, they neglect a whole collection of orderly procedures which may be more important than the minutiae of program format. This neglect is the more surprising since these procedures are employed, consciously or unconsciously, in all successful programs. They are a part of a broader concept of programming, a technology, if you like, that surrounds the much-discussed slicing of facts and interleaving of questions. This technology is not mysterious. It is available to anyone willing to work in an orderly and craftsmanlike manner.

This book, then, attempts to fill a gap by discussing a neglected technology. It does not discuss the finer details of this or that method of programming, nor does it debate the merits of one method over another (these issues, still far from resolved, will have to be thrashed out in the learning laboratories). Instead, it concentrates on such practical issues as the steps that precede the writing of the program proper, methods for testing your product, and ways to overcome some of the difficulties and avoid some of the pitfalls. It is aimed at teachers, trainers in industry and commerce, and anyone else who has decided that he is going to write a program. In particular, I hope it will lead to fresh efforts by those who have already tried program writing and have given up, discouraged or frustrated because the task posed too many problems. It tries to show that programming is, in large part, hard work and systematic procedure and that results come more easily if you apply your energies in the right ways. It leans, in short, toward practice and what is practical rather than to theory and what is perfect.

At this point, you may feel tempted to ask, "If programmed instruction is so good, why haven't you programmed this book?"

[2] A frame is one of the increments or chunks into which programmers divide information.

I have a whole string of reasons. As you will find out, I believe in trying to define one's audience and I believe in defining the objectives of instruction. In this present case, the audience I hope to reach is so diverse in its needs and interests that meaningful programming would be nearly impossible. In addition, I am opposed to programming just for its own sake. Program writing takes too much time and effort for one thing. And other, simpler approaches (even books) work perfectly well in many situations. A further factor that keeps me from programming is the difficulty of specifying the concepts to be imparted. Nobody has all the answers yet. I have purposely stayed away from the arbitrary lists of rules that some consider essential in programming because I think that each programmer and each program is different from all others. At best, I hope that when you have finished this book you will be motivated to approach programming in an orderly fashion and in a certain frame of mind. To that end, I have described programming procedures that have worked for me and for my colleagues. I suggest that you look at these procedures, try them out, and then adopt or adapt as seems sensible.

It seems fair to add that if you are looking for the complete and definitive work on programming, this is not it. Mind you, I do not think you will ever find such an encyclopedia, any more than you are likely to find a book that is honestly entitled, "How to Paint Masterpieces."

Even a small book such as this can owe a great deal to many people. I acknowledge gratefully my debt to: Robert F. Mager and Richard S. Hatch for many hours of stimulating discussion; my colleague Robert H. Kantor for his perceptive comments; David Cram who even took time out from a Hawaiian vacation to read parts of the manuscript; and Adrian Sanford of Educational Development Corporation, Palo Alto, for valued guidance in practical matters. The responsibility for errors and opinions is my own.

P. P.

Los Altos, Calif.
October 1965

Contents

Contents

I

Introduction

Programmed instruction arrived at an opportune time, a time when the demands upon our educational and training systems were outstripping the current means for meeting the demand. The numbers of students and the extent of material to be taught both still are growing faster than are the numbers of teachers and the aids available to teachers. As a practical matter, it is not possible to step up the supply of teachers and instructors in any significant degree. Nor can the gap be closed merely by giving the teachers the advantage of such tools as audio-visual devices. What is needed is a method that will simulate the crucial ingredients of the interchange between student and teacher and cause the student to take an active role in the instructional process. (A discussion of the role of "teaching machines" in this interchange is outside the scope of this book.)

Look at this interchange between teacher and student. What goes on? What is the end product?

In most elementary and high schools and in most industrial courses, the teaching-learning process involves the communication from teacher to student of known subject matter. It is an attempt, if you like, to advance the student along the path of knowledge. In higher education, it consciously includes communication of the facility to extrapolate from the subject matter for oneself.

In the course of this communication, there are changes in the student's behaviors (including his preferences, prejudices, and other attitudes as well as his observable activities). The skills the

1

student had to start with are recombined or expanded so that we can say, "He learned."

Ideally, the best arrangement for achieving this communication is to have one gifted teacher for each student. It is James Garfield's often-quoted "Mark Hopkins on one end of a log and me on the other." But this ideal rarely is approached. Compromises have to be made. Teachers have to instruct more than one student at a time, and, of course, some teachers do a better job than others.

Why do some teachers do better than others? And, for that matter, why do we need teachers at all? Why will a textbook alone not suffice in some areas?

We shall work backwards through those questions. There is no doubt that textbooks can be used alone in many situations, but they are probably not an efficient method of instruction particularly in levels below college, mainly because texts tend to be reference books rather than teaching books. Teachers are needed because they add something to the instructional situation. That something is what I call communication—an inadequate word for the teacher's function. The teacher can adapt the instruction to the student. He can involve and encourage the student by means of spot questions, confirmation of answers, and broader explanations. There is always an interaction between student and teacher, and when this interaction is positive there is motivation for the student.

Just how well these things are done depends in part upon the ability of the teacher. But even for the best teacher, the typical classroom contains too many students for the process to even approach its potential. The teacher must gear his presentation to what he senses is the average, too slow for the bright student, too fast for the slow one. Try as he will, the teacher cannot be sure at any given point whether he is getting through to all or even to a majority of his students. If he wants to check student comprehension, he must resort to a test—and then his knowledge comes too late unless he wants to go over and over his ground. Adding to his difficulties is the problem of the absent student who must somehow be brought up to the general level of the class.

Even if we take a positive viewpoint and label these difficulties as "challenges," they still keep the teacher from the more rewarding aspects of his profession. He is like a gardener who hopes to cultivate fine flowers and vegetables but finds himself forever battling weeds and pests. Just as the gardener has tools to work with, a teacher, too, has tools to help him do a better job—texts, workbooks, projectors, perhaps television. But they are not enough. The need is for something that will do more than merely extend old methods; he needs help, something that can take over completely in some parts of his work.

That brings us to programmed instruction. The teacher can delegate to programmed instruction some parts of his task, perhaps the routine part of his subject matter, the concepts that are hard to teach, or those that must be rehearsed until perfect. He can delegate such functions, knowing that programmed instruction is able to adjust itself to the individual differences in students' learning rates, and that it can guarantee that all students attain a predetermined level of proficiency.

With some justification, advocates of programmed instruction also claim that it can cut down on instructional time and that it can lead to uniformly higher levels of performance. But, in a sense, all these claims are secondary. The real strength of programmed instruction is that it is relevant instruction. Programming forces the creators of instruction to face up squarely to the issues involved. It compels them to make decisions about the end product of their instruction—what behaviors are acceptable, what is practicable. This weighing of each issue often results in the discarding of a long-cherished thought, motive, or concept. It also calls for a certain humility on the part of the teacher-programmer in that he has to accept that the student (or, better, the student's performance) is the final arbitrator of how and why a subject should be presented. Gone, in this situation, is the teacher's face omnipotence. And this is hard to take; it calls for some drastic and painful shifts in thinking for most of us.

Some teachers regard programmed instruction as a threat, and it is a threat for anyone content to teach inadequately. For the teacher who rationalizes his own inadequacies in terms of "stupid students," programmed instruction, with its intolerance of airy platitudes and breezy generalities, is the biggest threat in years. But for those who are ready to take advantage of it, programmed instruction is the means to add a whole new dimension to teaching. Merely by *using* it, a teacher can free himself for the creative work of the true teacher. By getting involved in *writing* programs, he can gain many insights into the instructional process.

From this point on, I will try to avoid sweeping generalities. They were included to provide a background for the rest of this book, which is devoted to the specific and the practical.

In attempting to be specific and practical about a large audience, one must make assumptions. I am going to assume that:

1. You want to write a program or that you want to have some yardstick to appraise what is involved in program writing and then decide whether you should be programming.
2. You are going to look elsewhere for detailed discussion of the theory of the different program formats. (You will find enough discussion of such issues here to enable you to write programs, but I do not pretend that the explanations are definitive. I want to show you how to *do* it rather than **how** to talk about it.)

2
Programming Today

If you are a newcomer to programmed instruction, you might be forgiven if you examined a program and came up with the following statement:.

"In a program, the material to be taught is broken into small steps and a question is asked at each step."

And it would not be uncommon (or, for that matter, unreasonable) if you went a stage further and made this assumption:

"To write a program, you take a written narrative of some kind, divide it into little pieces, and plug in a question after each piece."

But while all this may be forgivable, common, and even reasonable, it is not true. (However, I would not bet that it has never been done.) Even if the written narrative from which you are working has been tailored to your needs with the most exquisite care, this slicing and plugging technique is not enough. There is more to programming and pedagogy than a brisk recital of facts, even if the student is nodding after each fact.

The question is, how much more? What is the state of the art in programming? What are the basic ideas? What are the differences in opinion? And, as a matter of some interest, what is likely to happen in the future?

Precise answers to such questions are hard to come by. Much literature and a fair number of books discuss these issues without resolving them. It seems safe to say that all programmed instruction is based in some measure on learning theory. But as Ernest

5

R. Hilgard[1] has said of the various theories of learning, each accounts for some phenomena very well but is less useful in accounting for others. However, if one avoids the finer points of discussion, there is a certain amount of agreement on basic ideas and a general acknowledgment that some things are not done.

In this chapter, I shall start with a few assertions about principles or characteristics of programmed instruction and then examine briefly how they came into being. At the end of the chapter, I have listed four books which I suggest you read. Where you go after that is up to you. There is a large literature on learning theory, much of it confusing for our present purposes.

Characteristics of Programmed Instruction

Programmed instruction owes its potency to four characteristics and to a point of view that is often—and deplorably—absent from other forms of instruction. These are the characteristics:

1. *Small steps.* The material to be learned is presented in what have been called "optimally sized increments." (That last phrase avoids the question of how big is "small." We shall pursue the question later.)

2. *Active participation.* The student continually is being made to interact with the program. With each small step, a response is required of the student; in some programs, he cannot make headway until he has made the correct response.

3. *Immediate knowledge of results.* As soon as a student has made a response, he discovers whether he was right or wrong. (More on this shortly.)

4. *Self-pacing.* Each student has his own copy of the program. His rate of progress is determined by the speed at which he works his way through the program; he is not forced to wait for those slower than himself nor is he left standing by those more apt (not by the program, anyway). In some programs, the amount of instruction he receives is determined by his responses; the student who makes wrong responses is exposed to more material than the student who is performing satisfactorily.

[1] Professor of psychology, Stanford University, in *Theories of Learning*, 2d ed. New York: Appleton-Century-Crofts, 1948, pp. 14, 457–458, 485–487.

The different viewpoint mentioned before lies in the programmer's orientation toward the student. A program is—or should be—designed to produce specified changes in student behavior; the programmer has not finished his task until he can say "Yes" to the question, "Does it work?" He answers this question by testing the program on members of the audience for which he has written. At any point where the program fails in its purpose, the programmer makes revisions until his product does work. There is no room for alibis such as, "The student is stupid," or, "He is not paying attention." When a program does not work, it is the programmer's fault.

> Comment: Although there is almost complete agreement among programmers about the desirability of student testing as a part of program development, it does not necessarily follow that all programs receive this kind of testing.

Before you go any further, let me say that those four characteristics and the point of view have to become part of your way of life if you intend to program. Perhaps you should back up and read them again.

History of Programmed Instruction

There is a lot of talk about programmed instruction and the Great Educational Revolution. The fact is, programmed instruction is hardly new or revolutionary. It has some tenuous links with the ancient Greeks and strong ancestral ties with the nineteenth-century work of, among others, the Russian physiologist, Pavlov, and an American, Edward L. Thorndike. While it is impertinent to dismiss them in a sentence or two, Pavlov's contribution was to study conditioned (that is, learned) reflexes in dogs, while Thorndike interests us here for his "law of effect." This law said that the connection between a situation (stimulus) and behavior (response) is strengthened only if some success or satisfaction follows the response. Note the words, "only if." Thorndike said bluntly that if the connection between stimulus and response was followed by an annoying state of affairs, then the strength of the connection decreased. This principle of rewards through success or satisfaction has come to be known as reinforcement. It may occur to you that the ideas just mentioned have been used by animal tamers for centuries.

Historically, the next mention goes to Sidney Pressey, a psychologist who, before and during the 1920s, developed a machine that taught. Pressey's machine was essentially a device for testing the student by means of multiple-choice questions. After receiving instruction elsewhere, the student went to the machine which presented him with a question and a choice of answers, each answer corresponding to a key. The student selected an answer by pressing the appropriate key. A correct answer brought a new question. An incorrect answer, on the other hand, produced no effect other than to score an error in the machine; the student tried again until he located the correct response. In effect, the machine forced the student to respond actively and also gave him the immediate knowledge of results mentioned previously. Pressey established that his method produced measurable amounts of learning. However, he was apparently ahead of his time; educators showed little interest in his ideas and he had to set them aside for a quarter of a century.

That brings us to the 1950s and programmed instruction as it now is understood. If you have been delving into the literature, you will have discovered that there has been a tendency to split programs into two camps which bear the self-explanatory names of "linear" and "branching." The linear camp is headed by Harvard's B. F. Skinner; the branching camp is led by Norman A. Crowder. Spokesmen for each camp have been at pains to stress the virtues of their respective causes while deprecating, usually by implication, the disregard for "Truth" inherent in the opposition viewpoint. Within each camp there have been adherents to special causes whose utterances often have been attributed wrongfully to the leaders of the factions.

Comment: The two-camp approach is common and it is also so convenient that I will use it as a basis for discussion. However, in my opinion, it is misleading. I am encouraged by the "cross-fertilizing" that has become more apparent in the last year or two as programmers have used the method that seemed appropriate to a task. The various approaches strike me less as different schools of thought than as methods that differ in purpose and emphasis. Each method has strengths and weaknesses.

Linear Programming

B. F. Skinner is a psychologist better described as a "social inventor." He has long been concerned with the shaping and conditioning of behavior, in the widest applications, and he is the major proponent of linear programming. From laboratory studies conducted with pigeons and rats he has laid the groundwork of a science of learning and has extended his findings into the realm of human behavior. (It seems fair to add that although Skinner's name is rightly identified with linear programming, he is not responsible for some of the more debatable features. These features are generally the products of later—and, for the most part, lesser —prophets than Skinner.)

In essence, Skinner holds that a creature (be it bird, rat, or human) can be led to a desired behavior by means of a series of carefully structured small steps, provided each correct step is reinforced by some kind of favorable experience or reward. By rewarding the correct response to a stimulus each time it occurs, the psychologist makes it increasingly likely that the correct response will be given. For instance, he might give a food pellet to a rat each time a buzzer sounded. The rat can quickly be trained to go to the food hopper when the buzzer sounds. (You probably have trained a dog in the same way.)

For more complicated behaviors, it becomes necessary to teach a stimulus-response *chain*. In such a case, each response becomes the stimulus for the next response. For a simple example, the rat might be trained to press a lever to make a buzzer sound, giving this brief chain:

Stimulus → Response	:	Stimulus → Response
Press Buzzer		Buzzer Go to food
lever sounds		sounds hopper

Even with rats and pigeons, these chains can be long. Pigeons, for instance, can be taught to dance in intricate patterns, and rats can be taught to run through complicated mazes without error. These behaviors are built gradually, step by step, with a reward for each correct response.

Extending this to human behavior, Skinner's great contribution, a student is given a small amount of information (the stimulus) and then is called upon to answer a question on the information (his answer is a response to the stimulus). As soon as he responds, the student is given the desired answer. Since the program is carefully written at a level that holds student errors to a minimum, the desired response is usually a confirmation of the student's response. This confirmation is considered to serve the same reinforcing function for a human that the food pellet serves for a rat. (For a brief example of linear programming, see Figure 2.1.)

In the course of instruction, each student is taken through many small stimulus-response steps. And since each student does this individually, there tends to be a spread of completion times. It is not unusual for some students to take twice as long as others.

Thus we have the elements of programmed instruction: (1) information given in small steps; (2) active responding by the student at each step; (3) immediate knowledge of results; (4) self-pacing.

A program of this sort is "linear" in the sense that each student takes the same path through the instruction. However, the word linear can be misleading in that linear programs do sometimes branch; the student who indicates a need for more practice may be recycled through some of the earlier instruction or may even be taken via a longer path to the next stage of the program. This, no matter what die-hards may say, is not a deterioration from the strict standards of linear programming; it was envisaged by members of Skinner's group in their earliest efforts.

Some things should be noted here. The linear programmer tries to make each successive step in his program small enough to avoid student error; if the student does err, he merely is exposed to the desired answer and no other action is taken to correct his response. Because the steps are small, a linear program typically appears to move slowly in an inevitable progress toward its goal of instruction. The programmer's concern with an errorless sequence of responses usually relegates literary qualities to a back seat. While there may be some scientific gestures at these qualities in terms of reading-difficulty level, there is usually little

3. Anything which has mass and occupies space is called *matter*. The known universe which has *mass* and *occupies space* is composed of _____.

matter

4. Matter is the name given to all objects which have mass and occupy _____.

space

5. All matter has _____ and occupies space.

mass

6. If all the parts of a sample of matter look exactly alike when observed by the sort of equipment generally available to a chemist in his laboratory, the material is considered to be HOMOGENEOUS. In other words, all the parts of a sample of HOMOGENEOUS matter appear to be _____.

alike, the same

7. If all parts of a material seem to be exactly the same, the material is h_____geneous.

homogeneous

8. All parts of homo_____ matter appear to be the same.

homogeneous

9. H_____ matter is visibly uniform throughout.

Homogeneous

10. In homogeneous material any one portion is just _____ every other portion.

like, the same as

11. When different samples of a homogeneous material have the *same properties* and *composition* we call this material a pure substance. All *pure substances* are h_____.

homogeneous

12. If we measure the properties in one part of a sample of a *pure substance* they will be the _____ as those for any other part.

same

Figure 2.1

The sequence above is from Renee Ford, "The Classification of Matter" (Experimental Edition). New York: Center for Programed Instruction, 1961. By permission.

room or concern for the subtleties of style. These subtleties are hard to come by and one has to conclude that most of the psychologists and subject matter experts who have written linear programs have been concerned more with the science of the programming method than with the arts of exposition. Only thus can one account for the dullness which afflicts so many linear programs.

Branching Programming

Now we shall consider what has been variously called Crowder-type, branching, or intrinsic programming. (See Figure 4.7.) Two major differences in outward form are readily apparent between branching and linear programming. First, the branching program typically presents much more information at each step; where a linear program commonly gives a sentence or two at a time, a branching step may consist of two or three paragraphs. Second, the method for student response is different; in a linear program, the student often "constructs a response" (that is, he supplies a missing word, phrase, number, and so on), whereas a branching program usually employs a multiple-choice question at the end of each step (that is, the student chooses between given alternatives). Each response to the question is keyed to a different page (or, to use the jargon, frame) in the program. If you select the desired response, your response is confirmed and you are presented with more information, another multiple-choice question, and so on. If your response is other than the one desired, you are directed to material which explains why you are wrong and, typically, sends you back to try again or to attempt a parallel question.

For the moment, let us not debate the question, "How much information is a 'step' of information?" Then we can say that Crowder, too, presents information a step at a time, that he calls for active responding by the student, that he gives immediate knowledge of results, and that the student's progress through the program is self-paced. (In terms of self-pacing, the spread of completion times may be even more marked than with a linear program since a remedial path in a branching program may contain several frames for each one in the right-answer or "prime" path.)

At this point, viewpoints begin to diverge. If Skinner's concern is with the science of learning, Crowder's can be said to be with the art of teaching. Crowder holds that teaching is a process of communication. Learning he regards as a process far too subtle and variable to be the subject of a few generalities. In consequence, he concentrates his attention upon the improvement of communication between teacher (programmer, that is) and student. His stated view is, "To predictably achieve a desired result, one must either have an infallible process to bring about the result or one must have a means of determining whether the result has been achieved and of taking appropriate action on the basis of that determination."

Crowder makes no claim to such an infallible process. Instead, his followers rely on "a means of determining whether the result has been achieved." The means is multiple-choice questions. The student's response provides feedback to the programmer on whether he managed to communicate.

Embedded in that last statement is a clue to the two chief weaknesses of many programs written in Crowder's format. Before the programmer can be sure that he has communicated all that he intended, he must (1) ask the right question, and (2) supply the right responses.

Whenever a large amount of information is contained in a program step, it becomes difficult to ask a question that will test on all points; it becomes even harder to provide responses that will cover all misunderstandings.

These are not new objections to multiple-choice questions. But this is no place for reviving the old feud about the merits of multiple choice. The fact is that there are ways of arriving at multiple-choice questions that will go far toward satisfying Crowder's purpose. For example, the teacher or programmer can devise the questions and then determine what responses to use by seeing how students typically respond to the questions. My point of view is that these questions are not infallible gauges of communication. But when built with reasonable care they are useful for diagnosing whether communication has not taken place. They will tell the programmer, "Your message was not received. Try again." And when a test of this kind is made at frequent intervals, it becomes possible to say with some precision just when and with reference to what there was a breakdown in communication.

The controversy as to whether linear or branching programming is superior rumbles continuously and erupts spasmodically. Many studies have come up with results that say, "It all depends. . . ." Both methods—and derivations of both—have been shown to teach, but it is difficult to draw clear-cut conclusions from such studies. In fact, the person who is willing to condemn one or the other method forthrightly probably is talking from the cozy world encompassed by his own blinders. This lack of definitive statements hardly is surprising if you consider the range of interests covered when comparisons are attempted—surely few people will deny that teaching spelling to third graders has little in common with a refresher for graduate engineers. Yet both of these have been tackled with, as far as could be ascertained, a fair degree of success.

Two Spurious Issues

While the merits of one type of programming over another will undoubtedly be an important issue for a long time to come, the debate sheds little light amidst the enveloping smoke of semantics and side issues. (The image of sweet little old lady schoolteachers forced into penniless retirement by the wicked, impersonal technology of programming is a great generator of smoke screens.) But there are some things that should be said to keep the record straight. Even though they add little to what has been said already, they are in context right now and they may help you avoid some irrelevant arguments when you do encounter them.

1. *Linear programs have no monopoly on constructed responses.* Constructed responses (those, you will remember, in which the student generates the missing information) have an aura of respectability. But "linear" and "constructed response" are not synonymous, as some people would have you believe. It is true that a constructed response is found much more frequently in linear programs than it is in branching programs. But there is no reason why such responses should not be in a branching program —and even in the form of multiple-choice responses. For

example, given a problem in multiplication and a choice of responses such as (a) .434, (b) .435, (c) .436, the student must work the problem—that is, construct the response—before he can select his answer.

2. *Only an intrinsic (that is, branching) program shapes itself to student needs.* Here, the definition of intrinsic has become sloppy with time, with an unfortunate implication. Crowder himself defines intrinsic to mean that his programs adapt themselves to the needs of the student *without the intervention of an extrinsic device such as a computer.* This last phrase tends to drop out of sight, leaving one with the argument that a branching program is intrinsic because the learner, within himself, makes the decisions which adapt the instruction to his needs. This is all right; I doubt that anyone would want to make too much of the issue, even though the alternatives are commonly generated by the programmer. What is bad is the implication that other types of programs are "extrinsic"—that the path the learner takes through the program is decided entirely by the programmer. The fact is that a well-constructed linear program may have been generated initially by a programmer, working entirely on his own, but the final program represents the programmer's ideas as amended by student performance during validation—just as a branching program should. In fact, since a linear program often is easier to test with precision, the linear approach may well represent a truer picture of what the student needs than does a branching program.

The message of the foregoing is, "Beware of the man who claims to have all the answers." This is not merely the message of this book. It is also a part of the theme of one of the more interesting figures in programmed instruction, Thomas F. Gilbert. In some down-to-earth papers, he takes to task ("blasts" is hardly too strong a word) the learning-laboratory approach to programmed instruction and advocates some basic thinking about the purpose of such instruction. While he bases his thinking on the same principles that guide the followers of Skinner, his approach to the task is as pragmatic as that of Crowder. And out of this has come what might be called a third approach to programming known as Mathetics.

I say "might be called" because Gilbert would probably be the first to deny that he heads yet another school of thought. He more likely would maintain that he has taken the demonstrated work in the field of operant conditioning and then applied common sense to formalize a technique of programming. For the purposes of this book, a discussion of Mathetics would be confusing. But I would encourage you to find out all you can once you have tried writing your own first program. Besides his contribution to programming, Gilbert has had useful things to say about the analysis of training.

In addition to the major divisions of thought, the field of programmed instruction contains many subdivisions. This is not surprising. Every program writer, like every text writer, has his own ideas about how he should teach what to whom. For different tasks, different approaches may be appropriate. It is even possible to use only part of the techniques of programming and obtain great increases in training efficiency. For example, Mager and Clark[2] report a 65 percent reduction in training time by giving students objectives for a course and allowing them to structure their own course.

A final thought: It is hard to write a good program, and easy to write a bad one. But even a bad program may not be complete waste of time.

Recommended reading:

Cram, David, *Explaining "Teaching Machines" and Programming.* San Francisco: Fearon Publishers, Inc., 1961.

Deterline, William A., *An Introduction to Programmed Instruction.* Englewood Cliffs, N. J.: Prentice-Hall, Inc., 1962.

Lysaught, Jerome P., and Clarence M. Williams, *A Guide to Programmed Instruction.* New York: John Wiley & Sons, Inc., 1963.

Margulies, S., and L. D. Eigen, *Applied Programed Instruction.* New York: John Wiley & Sons, Inc., 1962. (Read just the parts that interest you.)

[2] R. F. Mager and C. Clark, "Explorations in Student-Controlled Instruction," presented at the 1963 convention of National Society for Programmed Instruction. Palo Alto, Calif.: Varian Associates, 1963.

If you wish further information, you might try:

Green, Edward J., *The Learning Process and Programmed Instruction*. New York: Holt, Rinehart and Winston, Inc., 1962.

Green's book has the virtue of being scholarly yet simply stated. Its drawback, in my opinion, is that it all but ignores anything which is not within the province of "pure" linear programming. The author's concern as a scientist to deal only with the scientific is commendable. However, it can lead to a myopic view of what programming is all about.

3

Preparation

The writing of a good program includes a lot of technique and a modicum of art, and it calls for the exercise of several specialized skills. Ideally, it is a team project since, excepting genius, no one man (or woman) is likely to possess all the skills. But do not let that stop you.

I am going to start with the thought that program writing is divided into three major stages:

I. Preparation
II. Writing the Program
III. Testing and Revision

Each stage is subdivided into a number of steps. Most of this chapter will be taken up with a discussion of the first stage, preparation. Nothing will be said in this chapter about whether you should use a linear or a branching format, but as you read keep in mind my suggestion that you make your first program linear.

Four general thoughts about preparation before we get down to detail:

1. Preparation is just about 100 percent technique; art has little to do with it. For "technique" you may substitute two words, "hard work." There is no substitute for hard work.
2. Beginners often try to omit this first stage by plunging straight into the business of writing frames. Be prepared to find that preparation accounts for at least 25 percent of your total time; give it less than that and you have probably done it less than justice. Time skimped in preparation is usually more than made up in delays during succeeding stages.

3. Do not bother about attaining perfection for one step before you begin the next. The process of programming may change your ideas about the topic you want to teach; it is very likely that you will want to back up and amend previous steps as further work clarifies your purpose. You will probably reach your goal in a series of approximations (and if you do not, it might be wise to ask yourself if you are not a little too rigid in your ideas). Important: It is fine to make changes, but be sure that you *write down any change you make*. Do not rely on memory to keep track of new ideas.

4. The discussion that follows is, of necessity, in general terms. You may find that your project—or your inclination—calls for more emphasis on one step, less on another. Do it the way that suits you. If a procedure seems important to me, I shall say so.

Here, then, are the six steps of stage I, preparation:

1. Select your topic.
2. Write a general statement.
3. Define your objectives in behavioral terms.
4. Define prerequisite skills, again in behavioral terms.
5. Write a criterion test.
6. Develop the content outline.

And only when all this is done will you begin writing your program.

Some of the terms above may be unfamiliar if you are not in touch with the jargon of programmed instruction. The explanation that follows may take care of that.

Step 1: Selecting Your Topic

Although this step sounds obvious, there are some things to be said. First, start small. Do not set out to program a semester of work or even a whole day of work. Select a single concept. I suggest you pick a topic that takes no more than an hour of a student's time. If you tackle something larger you may find that details kill your initiative. Stay little to start with; you can always write another program if you still feel like it.

Second, apply a few yardsticks to the topic by asking, "Is this something the student must know?" and, "Is it hard for him to get a good explanation from other sources?" If you cannot answer "Yes" to both "Must know" and "Hard to get" questions, the topic probably is not worth the trouble of programming.

Step 2: Writing a General Statement

By a general statement, I mean one that takes care of absolutely everything that is not specifically covered by steps 3, 4, or 6. The general statement is a catchall for every kind of thought you want to capture.

If step 1 above gave you the breadth of your program, this step will indicate its depth. Here, you describe as fully and as accurately as you can, the audience for whom you are writing. Capture in writing all the thoughts you have about the age and gender, skills, interests, and ambitions of your students. The skills brought to the learning situation by one group may differ markedly from the skills of another group and yet both may have the same training objective. To take an example: Suppose you want to teach your subjects to ride a bicycle on the highway. Assume that the subjects are two boys, one six years old, the other sixteen, and that neither has ridden a bicycle before. There is no reason why they will not learn with equal facility the skill of actually riding a bicycle. But when it comes to reading road signs, an important part of riding on the highway, the initial skills of the sixteen-year-old boy will put him in quite a different category from the six-year-old. Presumably, the older boy will be able to read the warning signs at sight, whereas the six-year-old may well have to be taught the meanings of the various shapes and symbols. The final performance may be equal, but the instruction needed will be different for each boy.

As you write this general statement, do not overlook other factors that may affect your students or program. Ask yourself the following questions: "Are there important limitations on their studying?" "Who, besides the students, must be pleased?" You may be able to say, for instance, that your students will not be able to spend more than an hour at a time with the program, that they will be studying at the end of a day of hard physical labor, or that they are not accustomed to studying or even to reading. It may be pertinent to include the thought that your efforts must be approved by a supervisor who will insist that the development of the topic be conventional or that it include terminology used only by a single group.

Your general statement does not necessarily have to be made available to others. But it is important that you be realistic with yourself by facing up to the issues and limitations.

You should be quite frank in writing this statement. Do not be concerned about its length or its literary style. Let your mind wander freely over the project as you write. You probably will be surprised to find just how many things can be said. This exercise will tell you a great deal about the way you should tackle your task. Right up to the moment when you finish your program, you will find yourself adding to and amending this statement as your ideas take shape.

Step 3: Defining Your Objectives in Behavioral Terms

Next, write down the finishing point of your program—the performance by which you judge when the student has attained the goals of your instruction.

This may look like a back-to-front procedure, but there is a reason for this approach. The final skill is something that all your students are going to have in common. Their initial skill levels, on the other hand, may vary widely from one to another, particularly if you are instructing adults.

Defining the objectives is, in my view, the most critical step in programming. If you abandon your project immediately after writing the objectives, your time still will have been well spent. By doing a thorough job at this step, you will overcome many of the problems of programming. I urge you to define your objectives not only with care but in considerable detail.

This step will give you trouble, particularly if you must cooperate with others in preparing your program. The writing of instructional objectives is a task that commonly is glossed over by using vague expressions of noble-sounding purpose, like this:

To convey to the student through a broad survey of the field, a thorough understanding of the subject matter.

In the absence of clearer expressions, you may have to start with such a statement. But do not try to write a program without a much clearer statement of what the student must do. Start by asking: "What will the student be doing when he is exhibiting this understanding?" "How thorough is 'thorough'?"

Words like "understand," "appreciate," and even "know" are meaningless to a programmer. He needs more precise indications of the performance involved. Again an example may help. Suppose we have to compare two men; one is an engineer who designs television sets and the other is a TV repairman. Both are competent in their jobs. In terms of their jobs, it would not be unreasonable to say that both these men understand television. Yet their levels of theoretical knowledge differ greatly. While the engineer might be able to take over the repairman's job, it is doubtful that the repairman could substitute for the engineer. There are differences between these two men and to describe those differences we have to be specific about what they can do.

It is amazing how many teachers and instructors say, "Yes, I can see how useful it is to have these careful statements of objectives for most courses. But in my course it is different. . . ." It may be true that objectives cannot completely describe the end products of some courses. But if you are teaching something to somebody, presumably you are working with some intent; presumably you, as a teacher, are exhibiting some behaviors that you want the student to exhibit; presumably you will want your student to perform in some manner which will demonstrate that he has learned something. If any of these presumptions are correct, then it is possible to write behavioral objectives.

There is some literature on objectives. The best work on the topic, in my opinion, is Mager's cogent and readable little book.[1] He suggests that you write objectives by asking three questions:

1. What will the student be doing when he is demonstrating proficiency?
2. Under what conditions will this behavior occur?
3. What is the level of acceptable performance?

Question 1 refers to observable behavior. Examples of observable behavior are, "Broad jump 9 feet," "List from memory four factors which. . . ."

---

[1] R. F. Mager, *Preparing Objectives for Programmed Instruction.* San Francisco: Fearon Publishers, 1962.

Question 2 refers to the conditions, restrictions, or "givens" under which the observable behavior is to take place. Example: "Given a radar receiver with a single fault in the input stage, the student shall be able to isolate and remedy the fault."

Question 3 puts limits on what is considered satisfactory performance. For instance, in the last example it might be pertinent to add the words, "within fifteen minutes."

A tip: In writing behavioral objectives, begin with an action word—cut, list, assemble, add, and so on.

Most people, when they first try to write behavioral objectives, seem unable to think small enough. They try to sum up the whole of their instruction in just one objective. That is the wrong approach. Instead, try to write an objective for every single skill that you want your learner to exhibit. If you write your objectives in fine enough detail, you should be able to write a final test directly from the objectives and say, "If he can complete this test, he is performing satisfactorily."

An efficient way of breaking down objectives into small enough components is to prepare what I shall call a "pyramid of objectives." In this pyramid, you start at the top with the over-all aim of your instruction. It is often useful to state this first level in general terms rather than in behavioral terms (see Figure 3.1). Then ask yourself, "What are the major behaviors needed to attain this goal?" The answers to this question, stated in behavioral terms, become the next level in the pyramid. Continue by taking each of the skills just listed and asking, "What skills are needed before this task can be performed?" The answers make yet another level of the pyramid. Keep repeating this process until you feel that you are dealing with skills the student can be expected to bring to the instruction. Make a full list of skills for each category; do not worry if you find yourself listing the same skill in several columns since this may be very useful later on.

Figure 3.1 shows a pyramid of objectives for instruction in reading a micrometer. The first level is a vague statement of purpose. The second level is a precise statement of the behavior required. Note the third major grouping of "Interim objectives." From time to time you will find that it is useful to build a special vocabulary for the purposes of instruction but that this vocabu-

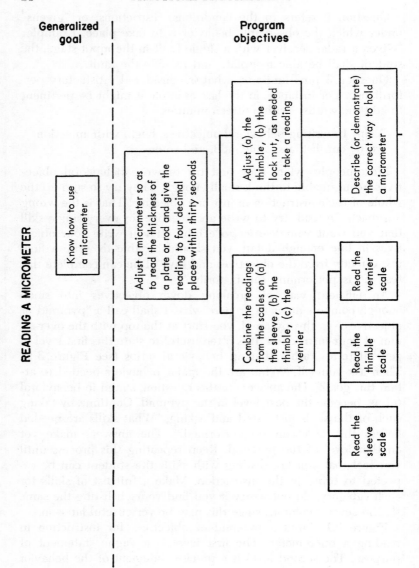

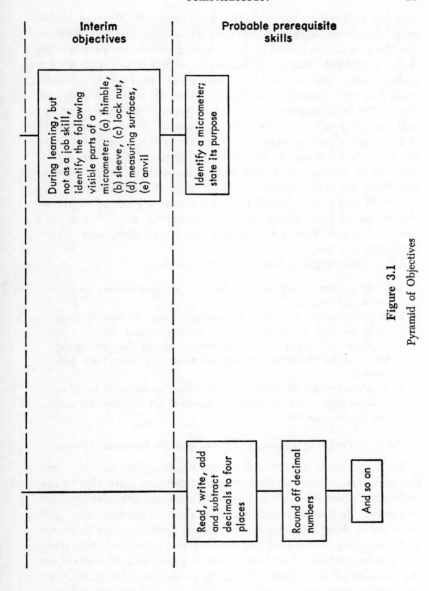

Figure 3.1

Pyramid of Objectives

lary has nothing to do with the final objective. Be sure to list these objectives since they form a part of your program. Notice, too, the title of the fourth major grouping, "Probable prerequisite skills." It is likely that a significant proportion of the students for such a course will be unable to manipulate four places of decimals. But since there is a doubt about this, err on the side of putting in too little instruction; you can always add to the program.

If you keep adding lines to your pyramid, eventually you will generate an objective which says something like, "Read and write the English language at the sixth-grade level." In many cases, this would indicate that you had gone further than necessary. But there are times when you have to go the full distance. Example: If you want to teach the operation of a piece of farm machinery in an area where many workers speak English but read only in Spanish, this question of literacy will determine which language you use.

All of the foregoing has a fourfold purpose:

1. It gives *you* a beacon by which to set your course as you write the program.
2. It gives *teachers* a plain indication of the content of your program and its applicability to their curriculums.
3. It gives *students* a plain statement of where they are going and enables them to measure whether they have been successful.
4. It gives *evaluators* a standard by which to measure whether you attained your objective—a standard set by yourself and not by an outsider.

Step 4: Defining Prerequisite Skills in Behavioral Terms

In the previous step, you drew the finishing line for your program. It was a clear-cut straight line, since you were able to say with some precision what behaviors were satisfactory as terminal or mastery behavior. Now you must draw a starting line. And since every human being comes to any learning task with his own unique collection of experiences and attitudes, this stage can pose a problem. Just how much of a problem depends upon the amount of confidence (factually based confidence, that is) with which you can describe the skills the student will bring to his task. And before we go any deeper into that, there is something that should be said: No matter how confident you are on this score, regard your list of prerequisite skills as provisional until you have proved them on a group of students. Your first list is an "armchair" list, a list of debating points, and not a collection of solid facts.

The defining of prerequisite skills resembles the previous step except that this time you are working with assumptions. If you charted a pyramid of objectives in step 3, it will be very useful here. You do not need to list layer upon layer from the pyramid; it is enough to take the highest line that is *not* included in the program. (See "Probable prerequisite skills" in Figure 3.1.)

Hint: Often, you will be unsure about where to draw the line. Follow the advice given in step 3 and err on the side of assuming that your typical student knows more than he does. Later on, when you test your program, it is much easier to spot areas where the student has been told too little than it is to detect the areas where he has been overcoached. When you discover that you have to add information, you can add it in small amounts until you get the results you want. If you give too much information to begin with, you will never know that adjustment was needed.

Step 5: Writing a Criterion Test

A little defining of terms probably is needed here. The criterion test is one that tests whether the student has attained the behavioral goals. It is not concerned with hard or easy questions; it has nothing to do with grading students. If your program is completely successful, every student will score 100 percent on the criterion test. Now it may be that you want to grade your students (and if so, I urge you to ask yourself, "Exactly why?") and that this calls for questions that will discriminate between one student and another. However, it has nothing to do with criterion testing.

Writing a criterion test at the stage of preparation will help you in several ways. For a start, it will help to sharpen your objectives and the list of prerequisite skills. And it may do a great deal in showing how to approach the subject matter when you start programming.

Be sure to write at least two questions for each objective and to include questions on the prerequisite skills you have assumed the student has.

If you have access to a representative group of students, you have now reached a valuable checkpoint. Give your criterion test to the students and see how their performances measure up to your expectations. The outcome and your reactions should fall under one of three headings:

1. Everybody performs precisely as expected. The students fail or succeed just as you predicted. They are unable to handle items based on your objectives but competent on the anticipated prerequisite skills. No changes need be made.
2. Most—say 90 percent—do *not* perform as expected. They display skills you had not expected or they fail to exhibit the skills you had listed as prerequisites. You must reverse yourself. If they are already competent in some area, you can delete this material from your program or, at most, you can briefly review it. If expected skills are absent, your program will have to include more concepts that you expected. (Before you do anything drastic, check the appropriate test items and make sure that your problem is not merely one of poor wording.)
3. The results are not clearly indicative one way or another. The message here is that your program may have to branch so as to offer more than one path—one for those who can demonstrate competence, one or more for those who need instruction. Note that this outcome is an indicator only, a hint that at a later stage you will have to watch for trouble. This point in development is not the time for firm decisions on issues such as this.

Step 6: Developing a List of Contents

You now have drawn a provisional starting line and a firm finishing line. It is time to think about what lies between those two lines. At this point, the pyramid of objectives becomes very useful.

If you have done it carefully, the pyramid's lower levels will contain a list of skills for which you have to ask yourself: "Can I assume that the student knows this?" If the answer is yes, put that skill on the list of prerequisites. If the answer is no, you must teach it in the program. If the answer is maybe, the concept goes on the list for inclusion in the criterion test, but is not included in the program.

Now we come to the reason for making a full list of skills for each column in the pyramid, even when the same skills are listed several times. When columns have skills in common, check them very carefully to see if you can structure the instruction in a better way than you have been accustomed to using. You may see relationships between one concept and another that had not occurred to you before. Ask yourself questions like these:

Am I using the most logical approach? Could I present this information in a different order and give the student new insight? Does each step build on what went before or on what the student already knows? Is each step listed necessary to attain the objective(s)? Are there enough steps to attain the objective(s)?

Which of these points needs most emphasis? What is interesting but not essential? Should it be included to keep the student's attention? Which points are hardest to get across? What needs extra practice? Where should reviews be inserted?

As you develop your outline, do not feel bound by your earlier work on objectives, prerequisites, or the general statement. Make changes if it seems sensible to do so. But. . .

If you decide to make changes, write them down.

If you merely make mental changes, you are throwing away a chief asset of the work you already have done. That asset is the usefulness of this earlier material as a measuring instrument of your program's success or failure.

Do not be misled by this apparent emphasis on re-examining the structure of your course. I am not suggesting change for the sake of change. Many subjects are taught in a particular sequence because there is an inherently logical way of proceeding from one point to another. So do not throw away hard-won experience, even if somebody else worked for it. But by all means be suspicious of inherited logical structures; make sure they meet the tests you, as a programmer, must apply.

Here is one more thought about experience. You may be programming for a learning situation you once experienced. This valuable source of ideas should not be neglected. Think back. What concepts gave you trouble? What insights cleared up those troubles? What approach worked well for you? Would you—with the knowledge you had in school—have liked changes in the order, method, or level of presentation?

The order and level of presentation that make it easiest to learn are not necessarily the order and level in which the expert stores information in his mind. And that is a point often overlooked, particularly in nonacademic training.

Final Caution

Those are the six steps of preparation. They are, in my experience, extremely important and often neglected. It is tempting to take short cuts around these steps, but if you cut corners you probably will take longer in total time.

There are a few refinements that may save you some time in the long run, provided you have the right kind of audience for your program. By "right kind of audience," I mean one that can vocalize its needs. In some situations, your only way of exploring the shortcomings of a program is the cut-and-try approach of testing and revision. But in many other situations, particularly those involving adults, you may be able to get useful information about the program before you have the first draft in hand.

For example, you may find that the students or trainees can help you with the very first step in programming—selection of a topic. Check with them. What are their ideas about which topics are "must know" and "hard to get"? (Their ideas about deficiencies in training may be quite different from yours, particularly if you are the instructor.) Once you have a topic, ask them what they feel they need to know about it, what aspects give them most trouble. Do not expect to get neat, clean answers to your questions. But if you remain open-minded, you can count on some useful indications of what is needed.

Another optional step in preparation which sometimes can be extremely valuable is the writing of core material. By "core material," I mean a straight prose narrative that covers all your objectives and does it (a) in the order in which you plan to present the subject matter to the student, and (b) in the language you intend to use in the program.

After all the work that has gone before, you may be tempted to skip this step. It is optional, but do not be too hasty about not using it. It may sound like more work, but it definitely takes you closer to rapid programming. Not only does it save time in the actual programming, but it can do a lot for good will and serve as a valuable checkpoint.

In writing the core material, you are, in effect, writing the text upon which you will base your program. If you plan to base your first program on somebody else's text, that is fine. I am not opposed to using existing resources (so long as you are careful not to infringe copyright), but you should be sure that the text fits your objectives with precision. If it does not, make changes as necessary, including deletion of nonrelevant material. That point about deletions is important. It always is tempting—and often it feels safer—to toss in that little piece of erudition. But if your purpose is to change another's behavior, this kind of showing off is out of place. Every concept included in your program should earn its keep. Remember the rule expounded earlier: If in doubt, begin by teaching too little rather than too much.

These thoughts may save you time in writing core material:

1. Do not try to turn out epic prose. Concentrate on covering all the objectives and on developing your points in the right order and at the right level.
2. As you go along, make a note of any good examples or test questions that occur to you. The reasons for this will become plainer in a little while.

And what does all this have to do with good will? How does this give you a checkpoint?

If you have on hand an expert on the subject matter or an audience that is mature enough to make some inputs, the core material is invaluable. Experts are usually busy men who do not have time to read and criticize an entire program. But they usually are willing—and may even welcome the chance—to comment upon a few pages of core material. That makes for good will. On the subject of checkpoints, I have found that you can get an early input from an intended audience by giving core material to a selected few and asking if all immediate questions have been answered. This yields useful information about what should be included in the program and what should be emphasized. This, in turn, calls for changes—and changes are much easier to make in core material than in a program.

4

Writing the Program

In the preceding steps, you have assembled the raw materials of your program. But before you start filling in details, it is smart to rough in the general dimensions of the program you plan to write.

There is more to programming than breaking a narrative into steps, even if your narrative is in the succinct form of core material. It is not enough to whisk through a recitation of facts and say the student is learning, even if he is nodding after each fact. Think back over your own learning experiences. Do you remember how much easier it was to learn when you could relate new information to what was already stored in your mind? Practice is needed. It is always helpful to know where you are headed. Efficient instruction needs more than facts. Facts are the essential skeleton of instruction, but learning is more effective when you give your skeleton the flesh and blood of examples and the life breath of style.

This chapter discusses the general format of a program and such issues as what belongs in the introduction, how much practice is needed, and where to put in summaries. You can help a student to learn in most situations by staying with two maxims that "everybody knows" and too few do anything about:

1. Teach from the known to the unknown, from the simple to the complex.
2. Tell them what you are going to tell them, tell them, and then tell them what you have told them.

The Five Phases of a Program

It is best to divide each chapter of your program into five phases, as shown in Figure 4.1.

1. An introduction that describes in familiar terms what is to be accomplished in this section of the program.
2. A review of any concepts that are essential to the task in hand. This review might call on the student to demonstrate certain important skills, or it might merely recall ideas for him in a summary.
3. The step-by-step development of new concepts, one at a time, in language which does not interrupt communication.
4. The "weaning" stage in which the student gradually is encouraged to display the full competence called for by the objectives.
5. A final summary and criterion test.

These phases are not all the same length. The introduction (phase 1), for instance, may be very brief; the step-by-step development (phase 3) will probably represent more than half of your program.

The five phases also differ in function, and because of that, they differ in form. For example, there is no reason why the introduction should not be a straight narration with none of the characteristics of programming. All the other phases will include program characteristics, but the form of programming will be different since each phase has a different purpose. This becomes plainer when the phases are examined in greater detail.

Phase 1: An introduction is needed because the student can proceed more meaningfully if he is aware of his goal. If you force him to "learn in the dark," he probably will feel frustrated; he may begin to wonder, "What does all this have to do with the course?" (This can provoke furious arguments with advocates of learning-by-discovery proponents. But there is no reason why a student should be unaware of his destination, even when he is made to experience the thrill of discovery as he picks his way to that destination.) In this phase, avoid the pitfall of displaying new words and terms. Many a sophomore has been discouraged by lectures delivered in senior vocabulary. Write your introduction in terms the student can be expected to understand. It is

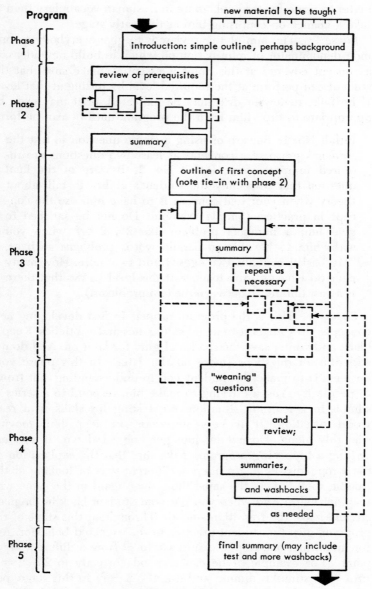

Figure 4.1

General Format of a Program Segment

better to write for the sophomore in freshman vocabulary than to take a chance on confusing him at this early stage.

Phase 2: The aim of this review is to give everybody a common denominator of information on which to build new ideas. If a concept covered at this point is essential, make sure that the student can perform at the required level by testing at that level. If he fails, review or drill may be indicated, or it may even be appropriate to drop him from the program until he can perform.

Pitfall No. 1: Beware of using a single question to test the student's grasp of a concept; at least two questions are required in most cases. Pitfall No. 2: Beware of the final question that tests only the student's ability to talk about theory when your real concern is to have him use the concept in practice. (Simple example: Do not be satisfied to give him a numbers problem like $2 + 2 = ?$ when you want him to be able to handle words problems such as, "My basket contains two eggs. I add two more. How many eggs do I have?" Any teacher at this level knows that there is a vast difference between the two problems.)

Phase 3: This is the program proper. In first developing new concepts, do your best to avoid side issues and subtleties. Keep it black and white; save the shades of gray for later on. And do not add difficult questions (more on this later). In this phase your business is to make the student nod in understanding, not frown in perplexity. You are trying to make him respond to a series of stimuli in a learning situation, not testing his skills in a real-world situation. It is very important to keep him moving smoothly along. Do not let him get bogged down. If you are writing a branching program, make sure that the explanation on the wrong-answer pages offers a different way of looking at the trouble spot. Saying the same thing over again in the same way may not help.) And when you put your student back in the main stream, make the transition smooth. Throughout this stage of the program, give the student practice in the expected behavior. Ask for more than one response, and ask for it from a different viewpoint. (For example, if he can respond correctly to $2 + 2 = ?$, turn your stimulus around and ask $4 = 2 + ?$) In this stage, pay attention to three points: (1) Be liberal with practice; (2) be liberal with summaries; (3) give your student options of going over material a second time or getting more practice before going ahead.

Phase 4: The exact position of this "weaning" stage is determined by the material. Here the student is being called upon to put his information to work. He no longer is being carried along with carefully graduated stimuli and responses. By this time, the first development of the concept has been completed. Now is the time for shadings of meaning, qualifications, subtleties, and all the rest. This is the place for the tougher, lifelike questions: make these the toughest kinds of discriminations you expect of him since if he can handle the tough ones, he will have no trouble with the easy ones. In this phase, if it seems sensible, you can combine two or more ideas in one question. And this is the place for reviews, perhaps washbacks (that is, enforced reworking of concepts on which performance is unsatisfactory), and, invariably, summaries.

Phase 5: The final summary gets a section to itself because it should outline the whole chapter (section, unit, or whatever you are calling it) in the newly learned words, terms, and concepts. It should probably offer backtracking for the student who is still anxious about his competence in specific areas. However, this opportunity should come after the essential part of this phase, the final test in which the student is asked to demonstrate the types of behavior set out in the objectives.

Perhaps you are acquainted with the expression "spiral learning." In spiral learning, the student first receives an overview of the whole concept to be learned, and then is taken in a series of passes through the material. Each pass adds more details, qualifications, or exceptions, until finally all refinements have been introduced. To put it another way, the student first gets the picture in black and white and then, in succeeding steps, the shadings are developed. The advantage of this approach in many areas is that at each stage of the development, the student has some feeling of competence. He is not "learning in the dark." He does not have to wait until the end of the semester before he can begin to explain to his friends what the course is about.

There is, as you can see, a strong connection between spiral learning and the phases of programming outlined above.

Student Responses

Earlier, I said that programming was more than just slicing a narrative into pieces and plugging in a question after each piece.

It is never that simple, but *if you have gone through all the steps* listed up to now, programming comes a lot closer to "slicing and plugging." Those earlier steps will have supplied you with the following:

1. A pyramid of objectives showing:
   a. the student's entering skills
   b. the final skills required
   c. the stages between
2. A criterion test
3. An outline of contents and, possibly, core material
4. A general statement

The first and second of these determine the essential subject matter. The second also gives you quite explicitly a string of test frames, check points between which you intersperse the learning frames. The third tells you the order of presentation, and the fourth should tell you a great deal about how you will carry out your task in terms of the level of language, the kind of examples, the amount of practice, and the amount of background information that the program must include. With all these things taken care of, you are left free to concentrate on the techniques of programming.

As far as the five phases described earlier are concerned: phase 1, the introduction, should present no difficulties. As noted, it probably will be straight prose narrative. Phase 2, review of earlier concepts, should not occupy you too long at this point because you are likely to make some discoveries about what belongs in this phase as you work through the later phases.

Quite quickly, you will be embarked on phase 3, the program proper. And here, particularly if you have written core material, you really can split your subject matter into concepts and call for responses from the student. The remainder of this chapter deals with the way in which you call for responses.

First, it seems desirable to repeat the four characteristics of programmed instruction. They are:

1. The material to be taught is presented in meaningful increments.
2. The student interacts with the program through active responding.
3. He receives knowledge of results after each response.
4. He proceeds at his own pace.

The first three are important at this point. The subject matter has to be divided into meaningful increments, the student is required to respond (usually by answering a question or performing some action), and he is told immediately whether he was correct.

I use the term "meaningful increments" although many sources use the phrase "short steps." The latter leads to furious arguments over how much is short. Meaningful increments seems to state the intention better, even if it, too, is open to interpretation.

Note that the meaning of "increment" or "step" covers more than the number of words in the frame. It also has to do with the amount of information being conveyed. For example, you might specify that the final performance expected of a student is to solve the expression

$$\int \frac{dx}{x + 1} = ?$$

In another case, the ability to handle this operation could be a prerequisite skill, tested on one of the initial frames of a program. That single problem might represent all the steps in a program, or it might be a single step.

Precisely what you will mean by meaningful increments depends upon the program format you intend to use, the audience you want to reach, and the topic upon which you have settled.

Program format is relevant since the increments in a typical linear program are much shorter than those in a typical branching program. (For examples, see Figures 2.1 and 4.7.) The audience affects your decision, too; as a generalization open to all sorts of exceptions, the younger or more naive your audience, the shorter will be the steps. (In partial defense of that last statement, I should say that you would be wasting your time in making finely drawn distinctions about step size if you were programming for graduate students in their area of major interest.

As a practical matter, the complexity of the subject matter and the assumptions you might reasonably make about entering skills would be likely to defy analysis. Distinctions about step size in such a case would better be resolved by trying out the program.)

Further and more useful help about step size and program structure comes from the pyramid of objectives. If you have given careful attention to the objectives, they will show with some precision the skills to be learned and the order in which they should be presented. The list of contents will refine this information further. Core material, if you have it, gives you the points you want to make, in the grammatical context in which they are to be presented. The general statement will help determine the level of language, the kind of examples, and perhaps the speed of presentation and the amount of practice.

By now, the purpose of all the earlier stages should be apparent. They enable you to resolve the problems in an orderly fashion. In so doing, you really can reduce programming to the relatively simple operation of presenting a point, skill, or fact, and then calling upon the student for a response. Without this division of labors, you are likely to find yourself utterly confused.

Format

A closer look at the way in which format affects the amount of information presented on a frame is in order here.

In a linear program, the format is typically this: A sentence of information (the stimulus) is followed by an incomplete but parallel sentence or problem based on the information. The student responds by completing the sentence or by figuring the answer to the problem. (More details will be given shortly.) The difficulty level of the response should be such that the student has an excellent chance of responding accurately, since the purpose of this exercise is not to test him but to make him respond correctly in the presence of the stimulus. The major hazard is irrelevant responses. Be sure that the response is relevant—that the word or words supplied by the student are the words you want him to learn, that the steps he performs in solving a problem are the steps you want him to practice. After he has responded, the student is shown the correct response; if his response is not correct, you may want him to repeat the last process, making the correct response. If his response is the one you want, he goes to the next increment of information, and so on.

In a branching program, the process is somewhat different. This is because the response is not regarded as half of a stimulus-response relationship; instead, it is looked upon as a check to see if communication has taken place. The increment of information may be much larger than in a linear program and usually it is said to be dictated by the inherent logic of the material. While this argument in support of size of increment is not unreasonable, there have been many sins perpetrated in its name. These

In a linear program, each step usually includes a stimulus and a response.	a
The program provides the stimulus; the student has to make the _____ .	b
_____ response	c
_____ Go to the next frame.	d

Figure 4.2

consist of throwing several kinds of information at the student on one frame and then basing the test of communication on only one part of the information. This is the aspect of branching programming on which linear advocates pour most of their scorn. And rightly so. But there is no real reason why a branching program should fail in this way. It is completely possible to present one idea at a time and to test to see whether it has come across. In fact, some of Crowder's own programs are distinctly "short step" in this sense.

With those generalizations out of the way, a closer examination of linear and branching programs now can begin. Some examples and comments should make things clearer.

Linear Programs

The basic format of a linear frame already has been discussed. Figure 4.2 is an example.

In this frame, (a) a small amount of information, an idea, is presented; (b) the student makes a response by providing a key word in a rephrased version of the information; (c) he checks his response against the desired response; (d) he receives directions on what to do next. (Normally, the desired response is kept hidden until the student has attempted his response.)

Note that this is an example of a "copy frame." That is, the student is prompted so heavily that even without understanding he is unlikely to make the wrong response. Much worse examples than this abound in programming. Copying frames have their

The general rule for multiplying powers of the same base is   **a**

$$(x^m)(x^n) = x^{(m+n)}$$

For example $(a^{10})(a^2) = a^{(10+2)} = a^{12} \cdot$ **b**

Problem: $(10^5)(10^7) = ?$ **c**

_____

10^{12} **d**

_____

Go to the next frame.   **e**

Figure 4.3

uses (more on this in a moment) but you would be wise not to expect too much of them.

Figure 4.3 is an example of a frame type which will be much more useful to you. Its elements are: (a) a definition, stated in general terms; (b) a specific example; (c) a specific but incomplete example calling for a response that parallels the one just given; (d) the desired response; (e) directions. Many linear programmers regard it as the classic method for introducing a new increment of learning.

In Figure 4.4, the elements are: (a) a generalization; (b) an amplifying example, calling for a response; (c) the desired response; (d) directions. This frame somewhat resembles Figure 4.2 in format, but one important difference is that it is not a copying frame. To make the desired response, the student must employ some information that is not presented in this frame.

> In most companies, the greater the skill required of an employee, the greater the financial reward to the employee. **a**
>
> Thus a scientist could reasonably expect more/less pay than a laborer. **b**
>
> ───────────────
>
> more **c**
>
> ───────────────
>
> Turn to frame 23. **d**

Figure 4.4

Figure 4.5 is really a glorified version of the format used in Figure 4.3. Its elements are: (a) a generalization that includes the diagram; (b) a specific example; (c) a specific but incomplete example calling for a response; (d) the desired response, including

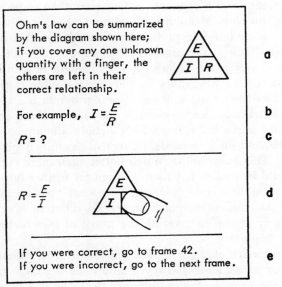

> Ohm's law can be summarized by the diagram shown here; if you cover any one unknown quantity with a finger, the others are left in their correct relationship. **a**
>
> For example, $I = \dfrac{E}{R}$ **b**
>
> $R = ?$ **c**
>
> ───────────────
>
> $R = \dfrac{E}{I}$ **d**
>
> ───────────────
>
> If you were correct, go to frame 42.
> If you were incorrect, go to the next frame. **e**

Figure 4.5

a diagram; (e) directions. I have added this frame to make a point: A diagram is often useful for presenting basic information or for providing the stimulus to which the student must respond. This may sound obvious, but the fact is that far too many programmers strive to verbalize what could much better be done with a picture. In your first program, you may be wise to stay with words as far as possible, but let me encourage you to experiment thereafter with programs that contain pictures.

A fault often encountered in linear programming is insufficient practice. Many programs contain frames in which the key word has been identified by the programmer and all that remains for the student is to copy the word. (As mentioned earlier, Figure 4.2 is an example of a copy frame.) In a copy frame, even when the information copied is pertinent, little or nothing happens for the student. Undoubtedly, he gets a little practice for his handwriting. But beyond that, the most that can be claimed is that if you immediately expose him to a situation in which he needs the newly copied information, you have improved the odds that the information will come to mind. If you want an axiom: Do not expect learning from a copy frame. One parrotlike response is not a learning situation. Meaningful, pertinent practice is needed.

One way of building proficiency through practice is by "vanishing" or "fading" the amount of prompting or cueing. In this procedure, successive frames give the student less and less help (stimulus) while still calling on him for the same response. The basic (but uninspiring) unit of a linear program is a sequence of frames which includes, in order, a copy frame, three or four fading frames, and a test frame which includes the minimal stimulus and a demand for a response. (A typical example is given in Figure 4.6.) This basic unit is much better than mere copying, but you should be aware that there is room for further improvement. If you want to ensure learning, you must provide practice by making the student respond in several different ways and by using lively examples covering the range of uses of the concept you are imparting.

This need for change of pace and breadth of practice is one reason for introducing you to variations on the basic frame pattern. If you examine the examples in the order in which they are

1.	An adult insect has six legs. Since an ant has six legs, it is an in_____. insect	Copy frame
2.	One way of telling if you are looking at an insect is to count its l_____s. legs	Prompting frames, giving diminishing amount of help
3.	An insect has (#)_____ legs. six	
4.	A spider has eight legs. It is/is not an insect. is not	fading to
5.	Because an ant has _____ legs, it is classified as a(n)_____. six insect	test or criterion frame

Objective: Given the stimulus ANT

student will respond INSECT : SIX legs.

Figure 4.6

Fading in a Linear Program

presented, you will see that the behavior called for is increasingly complex. (Or, to oversimplify somewhat, the answer is less obvious in Figure 4.5 than it is in Figure 4.2.)

Another reason for showing the variations is to introduce the thought that linear programs *can* contain multiple-choice questions (in Figure 4.4, for instance, the student has a choice between "more/less"), and that they also can provide for branching (Figure 4.5 contains an example).

Note, too, that a program does not necessarily have to present all of the relevant information. This already has been discussed under the heading of "Writing a General Statement," but it bears repeating. All students bring some information to the program; none is completely naive. You must make allowances for this initial knowledge, and you should make them methodically and in detail. For an example of such detail, see Figure 4.4. This frame assumes that the student is aware that the skills of a scientist are greater than the skills of a laborer. But the inclusion of a frame like this says a lot about the level of the audience for which the program was written. For an adult, a frame like this would probably be redundant. For, say, a sixth grader, who is unaware of salary differentials, the frame makes a point.

Figure 4.5 is another example of this same point. Check the assumptions for yourself. There are a number of them. In testing a program containing a frame such as this, you would have to observe the performance of your test population with great care to make sure that your assumptions were valid.

Arising from the above are a couple of statements that might even be called rules of programming, applicable to all programs. In a sense, they are refinements of the earlier admonition to "Teach from the known to the unknown." These are the rules:

1. Always build on established behavior. (You would not build a house without a firm foundation. Do not try it with learning.)
2. Hold the student responsible only for material to which he has responded actively and correctly. (You cannot *count* upon the student exhibiting behaviors unless he has been made to respond with these behaviors both actively and correctly. Because he can jump 3 feet, he cannot necessarily jump 6 feet. Because he has copied the spelling of a word, he cannot necessarily use that word in correct context.)

Both of these rules may seem so straightforward as to be obvious. Yet they frequently are neglected by beginning programmers.

There are many more issues in linear programming that you eventually will want to examine. I have said all I want to say. For a much more detailed discussion I recommend Susan Meyer Markle's *Good Frames and Bad* (New York: John Wiley & Sons, Inc., 1964). It is my opinion that your best procedure is to try writing a small program before you try the Markle book. (This opinion is based on intuition and is entirely contrary to learning theory!)

Branching Programs

The major aspects of the format already have been discussed: (1) Information is presented; (2) the student is given a question and a choice of responses; (3) he follows the directions given for each response; (4) typically, an inappropriate response leads him to corrective material and another attempt at the question while the desired response leads him to confirmation of the response and to new information. Figure 4.7 is an excellent example of a simple branching sequence.

There are fewer restrictions on the size of the step in a branching program. This has some advantages and some drawbacks. It permits the programmer to make his own judgments about the amount of information his student can absorb at a single try. It gives him more freedom to exploit the advantages of literary style. It may also be a much more appropriate instructional method for some audiences that resent the "spoon-feeding" of linear programs. On the other hand, large steps make it too easy for the programmer to rush ahead in developing his points, unaware that he has not put across some crucial issue, and often these large steps leave him without the means to identify this weakness.

For anyone with a writing bent, branching programs are probably much more fun to write. But I should advise everybody to try linear programming first, leaving the challenges of branching until the basic disciplines have been mastered. When you get to branching programs, here are some points to keep in mind:

First, let the logic of the subject matter decide the shape of the

A THEOREM IN
NUMBER THEORY

By Norman A. Crowder

In this sample we shall prove a curious little theorem about the divisibility of certain numbers. Before we begin, however, let's get our terminology set. When we say that 24 is divisible by 6, we mean, of course, that dividing 24 by 6 leaves no remainder. In the same way we would say that 29 is not divisible by 8, since dividing 29 by 8 leaves a remainder of 5.

Now here is a question on what you have just read. Pick what you think is the right answer to the question and turn to the page number given with that answer. The question is: As we have been using the word "divisible" is 11 divisible by 4?

	Page
Yes	7-A
No	10-A

Page 5-A

BEGIN HERE

You do not read this pamphlet as you would an ordinary book, going from page 1 to page 2. Rather, on each page you will be told which page you should read next. Furthermore, each page is divided into two parts, A and B, which are not read at the same time.

You are now on page 3-A. Turn to page 5-A to begin the sample sequence.

Page 3-A

Your answer was:

11 is not divisible by **4.**

You are correct. 4 "goes into" 11 twice, leaving a remainder of 3. Since there is a remainder, we would not say that 11 is divisible by **4.**

In our proof we will want to emphasize that certain numbers are whole numbers, i.e. not fractions. The set of whole numbers (including 0 and the negative whole numbers) is called the set of integers.

Which of the following numbers is an integer?

r answer was:

1 is divisible by **4.**

were using "divis-
" to mean "divisible
hout remainder". Di-
ng 11 by 4 leaves a
ainder of 3, i.e. 4
es into" 11 twice,
3 left over. So we
ld not say that 11 is
isible by 4. Now re-
to Page 5-A and try
problem again.

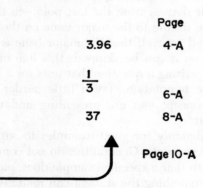

	Page
Page 7-A	
	3.96 4-A
	$\frac{1}{3}$ 6-A
	37 8-A
	Page 10-A

Figure 4.7

Simple Branching Sequence

From Norman A. Crowder, A Theorem in Number Theory. *Silver Spring, Md.: U. S. Industries, Inc., 1961. By permission.*

program. Do not make decisions about how the program is going to branch before you begin to write. Apart from resolving that not too much information will appear on any single page, it is unwise to decide ahead of time how much is going on a page. And remember that no rule says that multiple-choice questions must have some given number of alternatives.

Second, any time a student selects an inappropriate answer, assume that he has made an honest error. Do not abuse him or brush him off. Somehow the program failed to communicate. If it is possible to identify the student's error, then you must point out where he went astray, rephrase the explanation (since he did not get the point from the way it first was phrased), and then perhaps give him some practice before letting him proceed. You will be less prone to the common mistake of taking out your frustrations on the student if you keep in mind that when the student fails it is the programmer's fault.

Third, the questions used in the body of the program are not intended to grade the student's performance. They test to see if you have communicated with him. To repeat something said earlier: Programs are not guessing games.

Fourth—and it derives from the last point—in the body of the program, confine testing to the major issue on the frame. It often is tempting to tell yourself that the major issue is so self-evident that all testing on it can be skipped; this line of thought gives you an alibi for writing a question that tests for a subtlety or side issue. Resist the temptation. Try a little harder to find an example of the concept you are presenting and then base your question on that.

Fifth, seek diligently for good examples to support your presentation of the concepts. Generalities do not come through with the same strength that a specific example does, particularly when the example is something the student can relate to his own experience.

Sixth (and this one is opinion), it often is easier to write the "prime path" (the "right-answer" pages with questions inserted) before tackling any part of the "unprime" (the "wrong-answer" or branching) pages. The prime path comes fairly readily out of the core material and objectives since you merely insert into the core material all of the questions needed to test and practice the behaviors listed in your objectives. (At least, it can be *almost* as simple as that.) Once you have the prime path, you have a choice. You can go back to the beginning of the program and write your own version of the unprime paths for the students who do not succeed. Or, better yet, you can try out the prime path, with all its questions in place *but without responses,* on some of the students you want to reach. As they work through the program, take careful notes of the responses they make. These responses can be the bases for the alternatives in your program. (The alternatives generated this way may surprise you. You may even find that there is no need for alternatives in some places and that a constructed response will suffice. And if you do make a discovery of this kind, you will begin to see why I have little patience with those who are dedicated exclusively to either linear or branching programming.)

Seventh, avoid all unintentional clues in listing your alternative responses. The student should not be able to say with certainty: "That response must be the right one because the rest are absolutely wild." Or, "The third alternative is always the correct one." Or, "The highest page number always takes you to the right answer."

Eighth, avoid all tricks and traps in your questions. Stay away from words like "always" and "never." And tell the student right at the beginning of the program that he is not going to be tricked or deceived. (He probably will not be convinced because he has seen too many trick questions in tests, but reassure him anyway.)

Ninth, when you run out of ideas for a question—and this often happens when you are beginning to summarize a concept—here are some suggestions that may help:

1. If you are presenting material involving computations, give, say, four groups of three problems and answers and ask, "Which group contains an error?"
2. Present a group of steps in a process, randomly arranged, and ask the student to put them in the correct order.
3. If you have items that can be paired or arranged in order, give the student two lists (perhaps one list of concepts and one list of step numbers), and ask him to pair them off. Include some items that do not fit to reduce the chances that he will respond by straight elimination.
4. Ask him to decide which of three statements best describes the issue just discussed. Give him three alternatives, *all true*

but with only one a comprehensive statement. (The other two can be true statements about lesser issues.)

Tenth, do not overlook the usefulness of what has been called "confidence branching." This gives the student the chance to chose between responses such as, "I understand," and "I do not understand." The first response allows him to go ahead, possibly to a quiz to test his understanding. The second might lead him to a diagnostic test to see what his trouble is or it might even allow him to select topics for review. (This "do not understand" response could well be a convenient point for branching the student into a linear program that carefully takes him over the trouble spot.)

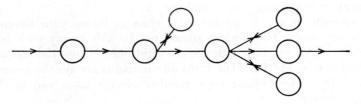

Figure 4.8

It seems appropriate to end this discussion of branching programs with some comments about the variations possible. This form of programming often fascinates a newcomer because of its apparently limitless possibilities for branching combinations. He envisages programs that will adapt themselves, with infinite subtlety, to many levels of ability. As a practical matter, if he makes the responses meaningful for a specified population, he will find that it usually proves to be unnecessary or extremely difficult to devise branches which are much more complicated than that shown in Figure 4.8.

Occasionally he may spot the need for remedial instruction that might add a sequence something like the one shown in Figure 4.9.

And when programming some trouble-shooting or decision-making function in which the student is to isolate some factor in a series of accept/reject decisions, a program might grow like the one in Figure 4.10 if it is to be adaptive.

One of the most useful systems I have used in programming

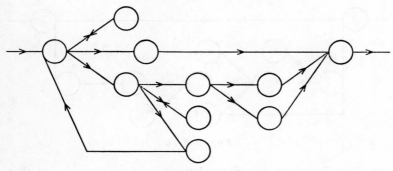

Figure 4.9

for adults with widely differing skills is the approach which has been called "criterion programming." In this, the student first is asked to perform at the criterion or final level of a program segment. If he can demonstrate this performance immediately, he skips instruction on the concepts tested. Then he is asked to perform at criterion level on the next group of concepts. Any time he fails to achieve the criterion standard, he is branched into in-

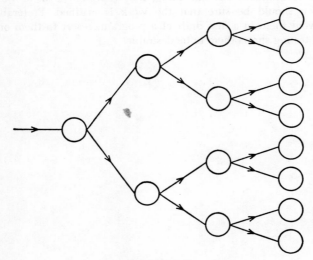

Figure 4.10

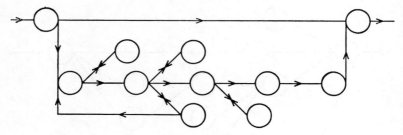

Figure 4.11

struction. Just how complicated the branching becomes at that point is determined by the subject matter and the audience you are instructing. The total effect is that another, upper level is added to the branching programs described above. In its simplest form, a criterion program is shown in Figure 4.11.

Two cautionary notes to end the chapter:

1. These "scramble diagrams," as they are called, are drawn *after* the program has been written, *not* before. They are a description of the paths available to the student, not a pattern into which to force a program.

2. Consider carefully before you embark upon these more complex variations. For one thing, they represent a lot of work. You should be sure that the work is justified. Preferably, avoid them in a first draft of a program; resort to them only if testing shows them to be desirable.

5

Testing and Revision

At this point you have completed the first draft of your program—objectives, program, and criterion test—but you are by no means finished. The manuscript before you is *your* version of what is going to change the behavior of somebody else in quite specific ways. You may be in for some surprises.

There are two issues to be faced during this stage of preparing a program: Has enough information been included? Does the information get through to the student?

If you have followed the earlier stages with care, you are unlikely at this point to be bothered greatly by the first question. You will have thrashed out all the issues in writing the objectives and the core material. Some of the assumptions made about what the student already knows may not stand up to testing. But again, if you have followed the advice given, the points of adjustment should not be hard to spot. You will have assumed too much rather than too little and the criterion tests will produce strong indications of trouble spots.

Your prime concern will be, "Have I said it in a way that gets the point across? Can the student demonstrate the behavior I specified? Did I communicate?" In other words, you will be looking at language. And you will be asking, "Are my words and phrases doing their job? Is language obscuring the point I want to make? Are the examples and analogies direct and pertinent, or are they misleading?"

Testing the program is the way to get answers to such questions. But in testing you get involved in human weaknesses. Today, Student A has a headache, Student B can think of nothing but tomorrow's football game, and Student C is in love. Tomorrow, Student A feels great, Student B cannot forget a fumbled pass and a broken rib, and Student C is deep in gloom because of a broken romance. And you thank heaven for Student D who is normal both days. The point is that it is not enough to test a program on one student. You need numbers, and, statistically, the more students you test, the better. The question now arises, "What is the minimum number of students for useful testing?"

I suggest that you can get by with about a dozen, provided:

1. You have carefully followed the early steps in programming
2. You carefully follow the procedure described below

A dozen persons may sound like a very small test population, and it is. It is a minimum, and, if possible, you should get a larger number. But testing yields diminishing returns. The first few student tests can do a lot in smoothing out your program. It quickly will become plain that some points have not come through, that some explanations are misleading or too difficult, that the order of presentation can be switched to fit the student's needs more closely. After even this small number of test runs, you will want to make changes.

Does it sound as though your first draft manuscript will get badly marked up? Well, it will. And since retyping manuscript is a practical matter, consider a practical approach.

Instead of typing a new version of the first draft, take your battered manuscript in hand and, for the first three test runs, "talk it" to the student, calling upon him for responses at all appropriate places.

Important: Stay with the script exactly until the student has troubles.

When you run into trouble because your explanation does not work, you should not be discouraged. You are about to get maximum benefit from this approach. Try rephrasing your explanation, or giving a new example. Get the student to the point where he can tell it back to you. And as he tells it, take notes on the way he says it because that may be the approach you need.

Before the next "talk-through," amend as seems necessary. On some points, the version hammered out in discussion with the student plainly may be superior; on others, you still may prefer your original version. I am continually surprised at the large amount of useful information that comes from these trial runs. It is important to take them seriously. If at any time you are not sure whether to use the student's version or your own, it is best to use the student's version.

With three talk-throughs and revisions behind you, you are ready to try out your fledgling program. This time, give it to three individual students, one at a time, and see what happens. Here are some points to watch.

First, the manuscript should be neatly typed. Your student is unlikely to have had practice in reading marked-up and battered copy. It is to your advantage to remove as many as possible of the obstacles to learning. Give him a program he can read with ease. (There is more about this in Chapter 6.)

Second, provide the best conditions you can get for studying. The reason is the one given above—removal of obstacles to learning. You would not expect best results if you made your student study the program on a crowded bus. An easy chair and a balancing act with the program, a notebook, a pencil, and a coffee cup are not a promising combination, either. Try to put the student in a room free of distractions, with all the things he will need within easy reach.

Third, be on hand in case the student runs into trouble. At the start, make sure he has all the necessary instructions. Have the instructions written down and make them as concise as possible. Give verbal instructions as well, preferably from a script so you say exactly what you want to say. Then move far enough away so that the student does not feel that you are looking over his shoulder, but stay close enough so that he can call you easily. Make it plain that you are not watching him by busying yourself at some nondistracting task. Preferably, read a book. That way, he will be able to see that your attention is not on him and yet your task will not seem so urgent that he will hesitate to bother you. If he does call on you, confine yourself to answering his questions. This is more difficult than you might expect. Volunteer nothing he does not ask about; as far as possible, leave instruction to the program. And, of course, keep a note of his questions and your answers for later analysis.

Important: If you find yourself telling the student, "That is fully explained later," action is needed. At the very least, consider adding a note at the trouble spot saying that an explanation will be given. Preferably, think seriously about changing the order of presentation.

At the end, give the student a criterion test.

You are now at a time for evaluation. You have notes about which concepts the student *said* he had trouble with. And you have a completed criterion test that *shows* what troubles remained after working through your program. Go over these points very carefully and objectively. See if you can detect what made him fail in the test. Was it the wording of the test? Was the question a fair one when compared with the objectives? (Remember that you are not trying to get a spread of test results. You are testing to see if the student can do the things you want him to do.) Look at the things the student asked about. How did you change the wording to get the point across? What did you have to add—or cut out? (Do not overlook the importance of cutting out words and ideas. If you have followed the earlier steps, there should not be too much excess verbiage, but stay alert for this kind of thing because it is a very common fault in programming.)

When you have finished cleaning up, you are all set to go through the process again with one important addition. This time, give your student the criterion test both before and after he reads the program. This use of a pretest and a posttest will begin to tell you what the student learned. You also will get some idea of which skills he had *before* he read your program. You may even find hints that he could do some things before he read the program and that he cannot do them after "learning"!

You may ask, "Why wait until now before giving pretests and posttests?" My answer: Until this point, you have been eliminating the large barriers to communication. Testing is a complex enough operation without trying to do more than one thing at a time. Thus I suggest that you make sure your message is reaching the student before you get down to subtleties. With a small test population of the type discussed here, the amount and kind of information needed for statistical analysis is not going to help. At the end of this test, revise again.

Now you can work on a larger scale. Give your program to a group of five or more students. Again, give the criterion test before and after using the program. If you have enough copies of the program, give it to all five at once. This time, let the program do its own work. Furnish no added explanations; instead, ask the students to make a note of any trouble spots so that you may discuss them later. When it is over, combine the test results of all five students and combine their comments about trouble spots. If all five fail on a single question in the criterion test, you have a problem. But there ought to be no real surprises at this time. As before, make changes where they seem to be needed. Now your program should be in fairly good shape for wider use.

Do not misunderstand me. This is not sufficient testing for all programs. But at this point you should have a program that will perform creditably. And you will have a program that has been tested more carefully than many that are making the rounds.

In general, a linear program is much easier to test than is a branching program. With a linear program, the programmer gets right down to details. He is forced to cover each point. In a branching program, on the other hand, it is easy to gloss over an important point and never even notice it until you find that the student cannot perform in the test. The test results may point out the trouble, but there is a fair chance that you will have a mental blind spot for some particular thought and that you will need a better tool than intuition to track it down. Susan Meyer Markle has described a useful technique for analyzing faulty branching programs.[1] From the viewpoint taken here the only drawback of the technique is that it calls for a larger test population than is assumed to be available. Her article is a valuable one, a fresh approach to branching programming and worth a place on your reference shelf.

[1] S. M. Markle, "Faulty Branching Frames: A Model for Maximizing Feedback to the Programer," *Programed Instruction,* Vol. III, Number 1. New York: The Center for Programed Instruction, October 1963, p. 4.

6

Editorial Qualities

This chapter is mainly a miscellaneous collection of thoughts about literary qualities, words, and other symbols of visual communication. But I will start by saying something about the use of editors.

I should make it plain that I am not talking about executive-type Editors with a capital "E"; I want to discuss the little-e editor, the person who wields a black pencil on your pellucid prose. The distinction is important because this editor's role is much misunderstood and much abused (in two senses of the word).

An editor can be of great help to you in program writing, and he can be particularly useful when you have just finished the first draft. At that point, a good editor can save you a lot of testing and revising.

A good editor is a literary tailor who can nip and tuck and slash and seam and shrink the writing of another in a fashion that adds significantly to the clarity of the prose and yet leaves the writer contented that "not a word was changed." This calls for unusual qualities in the editor; his character must combine, in approximately equal portions, an arrogance that allows him to cut through verbiage to the heart of a presentation, together with a humility that permits him to retain the style of the writer within the edited manuscript. The second quality, humility, is, in my opinion, all too often missing. And the editor without it runs the risk that his scissors and pencil will hack the life out of any manuscript.

Editing of this kind is a distinct professional skill—and hard to find. If you find a man who qualifies, hold onto him.

We should return now to practical matters. You have a program, but you do not have an editor. And you are not about to get professional help. What then?

The second best course is to ask a sympathetic friend, whose opinion you value, to look over your manuscript. But before you hand over the manuscript, put it away for at least a week and then go over it as dispassionately as your constitution will permit. In this process, keep asking yourself these questions:

1. In essence, what is this frame about?
2. Does my message come through, or have I obscured it in verbiage, jumbled thoughts, misplaced verbal tricks, or inept wording?
3. Does each question or response perform its function?
4. Is the chain of logic complete, or have I made unjustifiable assumptions about the student's skills?
5. Is there enough practice?
6. Are there enough summaries?

And a final word to the author from those wise old Greeks: If some phrase, sentence, or paragraph particularly takes your fancy, you probably would be wise to strike it out.

If your manuscript has passed all these tests, you then deliver it to your friend's keeping. He, too, should ask those same questions (changing the pronouns, of course), and he should follow one more rule:

At all times, insist that the argument be based on what already has been said in the program or listed in the general statement as a prerequisite.

This rule, one of the most useful and important in programming, often is overlooked. Programmers are always looking for miracles. Before an explanation has been made available they are trying to make the student apply it. To restate that rule a little:

Never look ahead for an explanation. If you need the explanation to make a response, then it should have appeared before the need arose.

When your editor-friend has completed his task he may have doubts, criticisms, or queries. These should not be shrugged off. The mere fact that he raises them means that you must weigh each one carefully and, probably, that you must act. After all, here is the first audience to which your program has been exposed.

Incidentally, do not underestimate the difficulty of accepting a friend's criticisms. It is hard, even if you have followed the advice given above and found a friend who is sympathetic to your intentions.

Having introduced the other person who is going to help and advise you, I now must make a few generalizations. There may be morals in these generalizations for you and your editor-friend.

For many subject-matter experts, a kind of split personality seems to be an occupational hazard. One would never guess from their writings what bright and interesting people so many of them are. When *talking* about their subject, their words are vigorous, even entertaining, and readily understood. But when they put their thoughts on paper, vigor vanishes and clarity is submerged in "weasel-worded" precision. It seems that their efforts are directed toward entrenchment against the attacks of overly critical peers rather than toward the building of paths of communication that will lead students to new knowledge and understanding.

To be fair, much has been done about this problem in recent years, especially in books used in public schools. But there is still a long way to go in some areas, notably in texts used at the technician level or above. All too often, textbooks are, in fact, reference books rather than instruction books. The student who seeks an explanation in these books finds that the "explanation" brings in its wake a whole series of new words and topics calling for explanation.

Authors defend this practice by claiming that accuracy is their target and that it is impossible to be accurate and precise without using the language of the subject. The real reason, probably not even recognized by these apologists, is twofold: (1) Keeping the material at the definitive level is respectable, customary, and relatively easy. (2) Making books both simple enough and accurate enough to be respectable involves a great deal more work.

This is not to say that the standard work on quantum mechanics should be written for sixth graders. But it *is* to say that an electronics course for would-be TV repairmen probably has no right declaiming that a tube's performance "varies in a nonlinear manner." There are other ways of saying the same thing just as precisely, just as accurately, and certainly a good deal more plainly.

Let nobody extend this argument into one favoring the abolition of all technical phrases from technical texts. It is quite true that if a man is to operate in some technical area he must learn the special language of the technique (unless he intends to pursue his occupation on some desert isle). What is being decried is the use of technical jargon almost, it seems, for the sake of jargon.

If you are writing a linear program, the decision to use some technical word or phrase presents few problems. You can make the decision ahead of time that you will present this key word or phrase and you can define and practice a single word with no difficulty. In a branching program, on the other hand, there is always a danger that your preliminary planning will not be specific enough to identify the word or phrase. Even if it is identified, there is a further danger that it will be buried or glossed over in a fashion that does not bring it home to the student. You can guard against this quite simply: Define the word or phrase carefully the first time you use it in the program and also use some synonyms. The next few times you use the word or phrase, put in a synonym in parentheses. (If the word is really vital, draw special attention to it by making it the subject of a response or even a series of responses.) Then, once you are confident that the student understands it, use the special word or phrase to the exclusion of all synonyms, taking no heed of variation or other literary niceties. (I hope it will have occurred to you that what is being advocated here is the use of the vanishing or fading technique.)

While on the subject of whether to ban or to use certain words, a brief remark about contractions is in order.

Be sparing in the use of contractions.

Contractions are a dangerous hazard. A student probably uses contractions in his speech, but it is equally probable that he cannot read them. Apart from the few common contractions—*it's, can't, don't, I'll, you're,* and the like—it is safer to spell out. Contractions such as *they're* and *this'll* are most likely outside the student's reading vocabulary. Even if he is familiar with them, he may have to stop and think about them. Stopping and thinking is fine, so long as it is confined to the task in hand; it should not be concerned with the mere mechanics of communication.

You also would be wise to stay away from the vernacular and colloquialisms. Nothing in prose is as dead as yesterday's slang.

And if I may add a personal plea: Stay away from sign writer's shorthand. Such corruptions as *thru, lo,* and *hi,* have no place in a program.

Here is another important point in this context: Some day your program may be used to instruct foreign students for whom English is a second language. Often, since such students comprehend written English more readily than they absorb the spoken word, a written program is a valuable teacher. But they will be unable to comprehend the vernacular.

For the same kinds of reasons, avoid such words as *arbitrarily, simultaneously,* and *juxtaposition.* Without making a rule of it, five-syllable words should be avoided. They defeat your purpose if they are outside the precise vocabulary of your student (and note that word "precise"). I feel almost apologetic for bringing up the subject since this is plainly a field for common sense, but it seems to be worth repeating: When in doubt, leave out. Err on the side of simplicity, rather than on the side of tongue-twisting pomposity.

Again, try not to use the phrases with which the would-be scholars are apt to embellish their conversation. A very simple instance is a phrase such as *in general.* As it is widely used in everyday conversation, it means "in the main, usually," or, to say it yet another way, "with reference to most cases." As it is used by those of scientific bent, it means "with reference to all spoken of."

Words are your chief weapon in the battle for understanding, but the artist can be your major ally in this endeavor. There are a number of artistic-type tactics you can employ to make your words more effective.

First, consider the editorial make-up of a page. There is not much freedom if you are using a linear program. But if you are writing a branching program, your page, regardless of content, is going to look more interesting if you get some color in it and by *color* I do not necessarily mean the use of inks of differing hues. What I am urging is that you avoid making a page that is all one shade of gray. Get some shadings in your grays; aim for blacks and whites and the page will have much more impact. As a bonus, it will probably be easier to read because it will save the student some of the problems of organizing his thinking processes. How to do it? You can get this kind of color on a page if you:

1. Set out your material point by point whenever possible. If you are using a typewritten format, use single-line space and indent on both sides, to get the kind of effect being used here.

2. Keep your paragraphs brief. If you follow the rule of having no more than one idea in a paragraph, the way that most newspapers do, you can ignore the rest of the paragraphing rules of the grammar book.

3. Keep your writing line fairly short. A writing line of ten words is plenty. A line of 4½ inches is a good standard.

4. In a branching program, restrict each page or frame to a maximum or six paragraphs. For paragraphs, fewer is better. (In other words, remember that you are presenting information in "meaningful increments.")

5. Use separate paragraphs for definitions and any other statements that call for special emphasis.

6. Remember that it pays to be generous with white space around type. This is just another way of saying that the sharper contrast of blacks and whites is more acceptable to the eye than is a gray wash.

If you have art work in your program—and pictures are very useful for telling some kinds of stories—there are one or two things you should keep in mind.

Try to keep your page lively and interesting without making it look "busy." One way of doing this is to use asymmetry rather than symmetry in laying out the page. For instance, if you have two pieces of art to put on one page and they are referred to separately, you might consider putting one at upper right with type wrapped around it and the other almost at the bottom of the page and at the left, again with type wrapped around it (see Figure 6.1A and B).

If you have just one piece of art and a page that is fairly full, the best position for the art is probably at upper right, with type around it (see Figure 6.1C and D). Why? Try it yourself. As you can see, it is easier to begin reading at upper left in the accustomed place than to start in the middle of the page as you must if you put the picture at upper left.

In contradictory fashion, a picture low on the page can go at left; the balance of the page is not upset and, for obscure reasons, it no longer seems hard to read from mid-page (see Figure 6.1E and F). Again, if you do not believe it, try it for yourself.

One thing to avoid is a small amount of type above a picture. Unless the art is at least one third of the way down the page, put the type beneath it (see Figure 6.1G and H). Art work has much more visual impact than has type; a skimpy line or two of type above the art is likely to be overlooked by the reader.

Another item in this category: Any "administrative text"—pagination, bottom of page instructions to the reader, any other instruction that appears regularly—should be presented in the same form each time it is used and should, as far as seems sensible, be placed in the same position on each page. This way, the reader will become accustomed to the instruction and its position and will read the instruction with the least possible distraction.

I want to add one final thought, and it is connected with the foregoing only in an indirect way. It is this: By the time you have gone through all the stages of program writing listed here, there is a strong possibility that you will loathe your program.

It may be that you will disprove my theory and that your enthusiasm will burn more and more brightly as you wind up your task. But it is my experience—and I have checked with many friends in many aspects of the "writing business"—that when you have finished the changing, switching, and compromising involved in a writing task of any size, you will be pretty much soured on the whole project. This is especially true of programming, where decisions and changes are so often in the direction of simplifying; by the time you are through, you are likely to feel that what you have is so simple as to be obvious. You probably will mutter to yourself, "All that work for so little!"

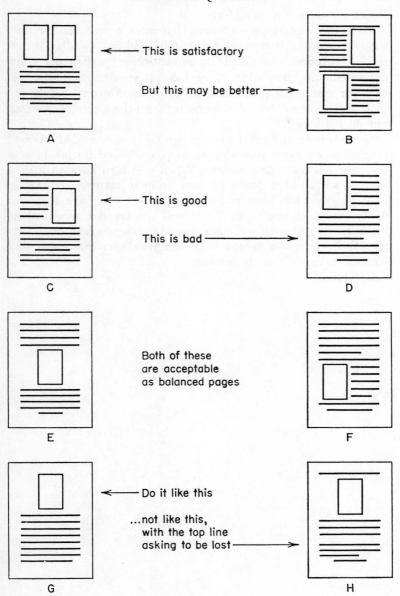

Figure 6.1

Let me offer some comfort.

First, the supreme compliment that most people can pay any written work is, "It is so simple that I could have written it myself." The fact is that simplicity in exposition, particularly when done with full knowledge of the facts, is very hard to attain. It calls for continued distillation of thoughts. You can safely say that any commentator who comes up with the quote above cannot do it himself.

Second, time, the great healer, also takes care of disillusioned programmers. Keep your doubts to yourself and do not look at the program for a few months. When you turn back to it, you may be surprised to find that your opinion has changed. When your program has been put to work, when you have seen students busily responding to the stimuli you created, when others begin to congratulate you, then you are going to feel much better. And when you reread your program, you may even find yourself saying, "That is not bad!"

Good luck!

Index